Fingerpower®
Level Two

Effective Technic for All Piano Methods

By John W. Schaum
Edited by Wesley Schaum

FOREWORD

Schaum Fingerpower® exercises are designed to strengthen all five fingers of both hands. Equal hand development is assured by the performance of the same patterns in each hand. The exercises are short and easily memorized. This enables the student to focus his/her efforts on technical benefits, listening attentively and playing with a steady beat. Also see **Directions for Use of Slurs** on page 2.

A measure number (enclosed in a small box) is included at the beginning of each system of music. This makes it easier to locate measures during the lesson and for written practice assignments.

The exercises become progressively more difficult as the student moves through the book. This makes the exercises an ideal companion to a method book at the same level. The series consists of seven books, Primer Level through Level 6.

PRACTICE SUGGESTIONS

To derive the full benefit from these exercises, they should be played with a firm, solid finger action. **Listen carefully while practicing**. Try to play **each finger equally loud**. Each hand should also play equally loud. It is also important to be aware of the feeling in your fingers and hands during practice.

Each exercise should be practiced four or five times daily, starting at a slow tempo and gradually increasing the tempo as proficiency improves. Several previously learned exercises should be reviewed each week as part of regular practice.

PLAYBACK+
Speed • Pitch • Balance • Loop

To access audio visit:
www.halleonard.com/mylibrary

3814-5585-5370-8564

ISBN 978-1-936098-92-7

Schaum

EXCLUSIVELY DISTRIBUTED BY

HAL•LEONARD®

Copyright © 1968, 2005 by Schaum Publications, Inc.
International Copyright Secured   All Rights Reserved

Visit Hal Leonard Online at
www.halleonard.com

Contact us:
Hal Leonard
7777 West Bluemound Road
Milwaukee, WI 53213
Email: info@halleonard.com

In Europe, contact:
Hal Leonard Europe Limited
42 Wigmore Street
Marylebone, London, W1U 2RN
Email: info@halleonardeurope.com

In Australia, contact:
Hal Leonard Australia Pty. Ltd.
4 Lentara Court
Cheltenham, Victoria, 3192 Australia
Email: info@halleonard.com.au

CONTENTS

DIRECTIONS for USE of SLURS:

Slurs may be used in several different ways at this level, according to teacher preference:

1. Slurs are used to **show similarity of patterns**, as an aid to learning the exercises. Play legato throughout. Do *not* lift the hand at the end of each slur.

2. Phrases may be observed by making a **slight accent at the beginning of each slur** or a small crescendo and diminuendo through each slur. (Hands are *not* lifted at the end of each slur.)

3. A "lift," "breath" or "break" may be made at the end of each slur, being careful not to interrupt the rhythm. The method of phrase attack and release is left to the preference of the teacher.

The exercises in this book offer an excellent opportunity to teach phrase attack and phrase release. The exercises are short and the note patterns are easily learned, so the pupil is free to focus on phrasing. Both hands have identical slur patterns and the phrase groups are consistent throughout each exercise, making the phrasing easy.

If desired, the pupil could learn the exercises *at first without phrasing*, later adding the phrasing as each exercise is reviewed.

ABOUT THE AUDIO

To access the accompanying audio, go to **www.halleonard.com/mylibrary** and enter the code found on the first page of this book. This will grant you instant access to every example.

There are two tracks for each exercise:
1. Slow practice tempo
2. Performance tempo

The solo part is emphasized on the practice track. The accompaniment is emphasized on the performance track. There are two extra count-in measures before each track.

Follow these three steps for practice variety. At first, the steps should be done with the slow practice tempo. The same steps may be used again at the performance tempo.
1. Student plays right hand only
2. Student plays left hand only
3. Student plays both hands together

1. Etude in Steps and Skips

TRACK 1: Slow
TRACK 2: Tempo

3

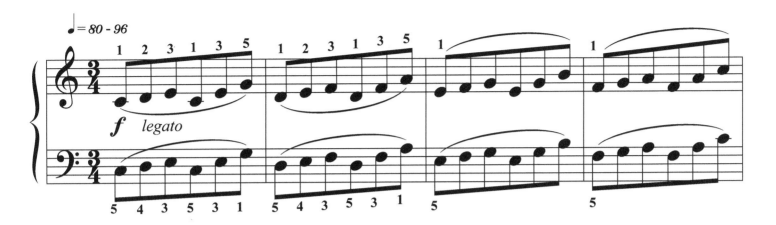

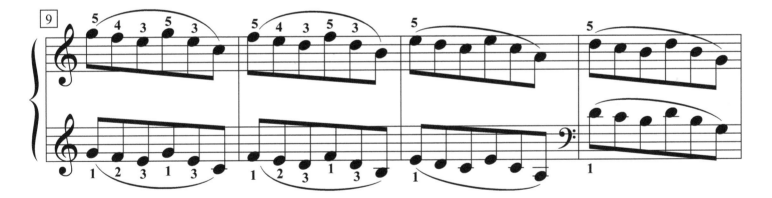

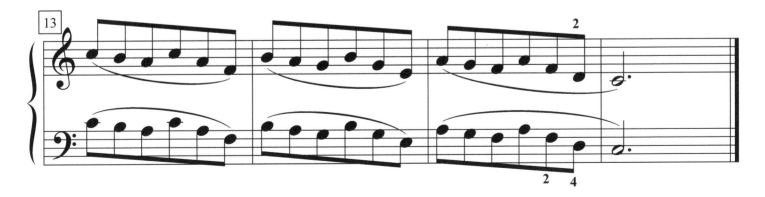

Special Assignment: Also play the above *Etude* in the following rhythm:

etc.

4

2. Etude in 6/8 Time

TRACK 3: Slow
TRACK 4: Tempo

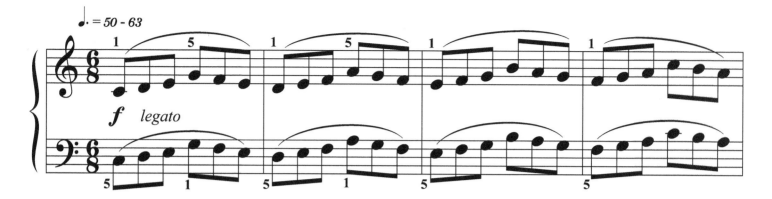

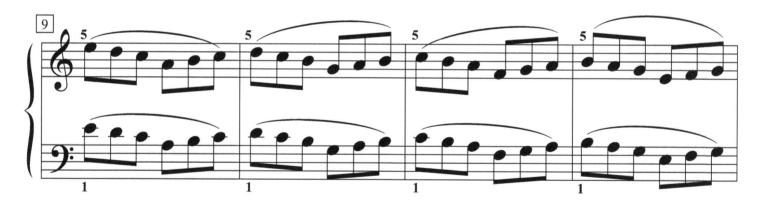

Special Assignment: Also play the above *Etude* in the following rhythm:

etc.

3. Alternating Hands

TRACK 5: Slow
TRACK 6: Tempo

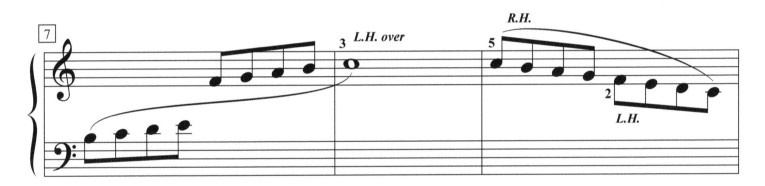

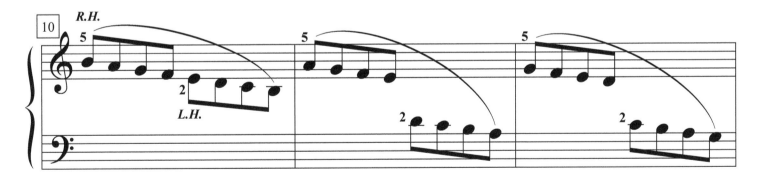

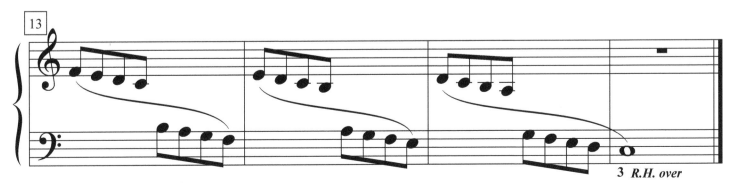

Note: Play all eighth notes VERY EVENLY.

4. Contrary Motion

TRACK 7: Slow
TRACK 8: Tempo

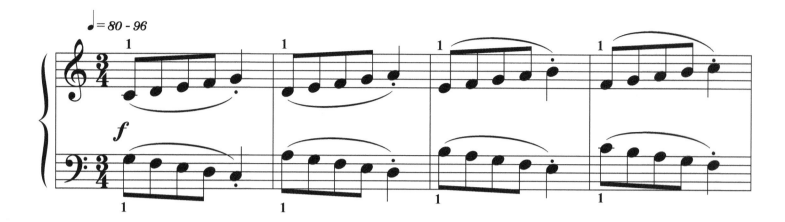

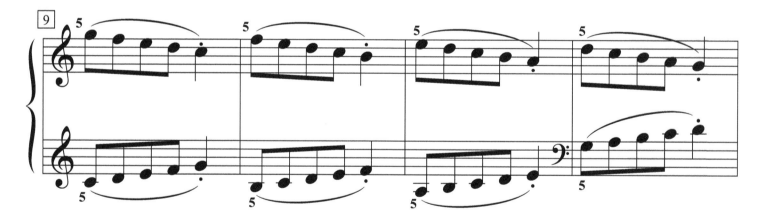

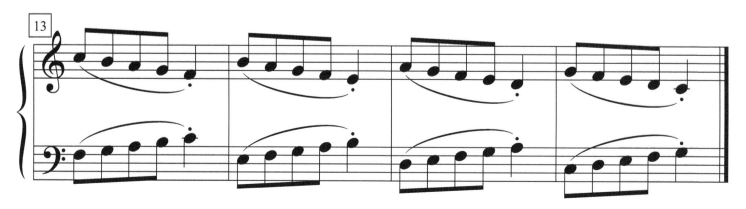

5. Mixed Interval Etude

TRACK 9: Slow
TRACK 10: Tempo

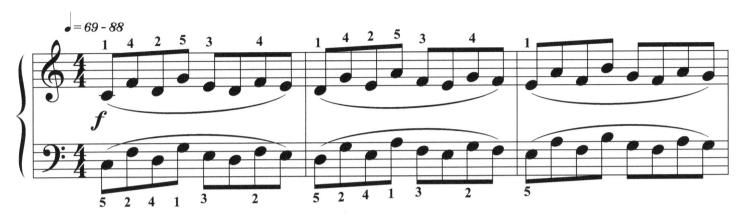

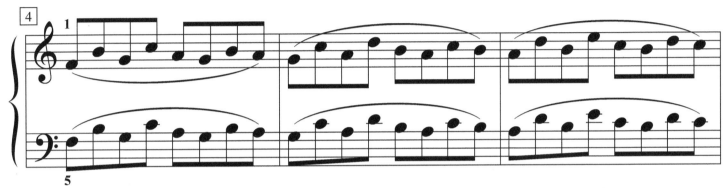

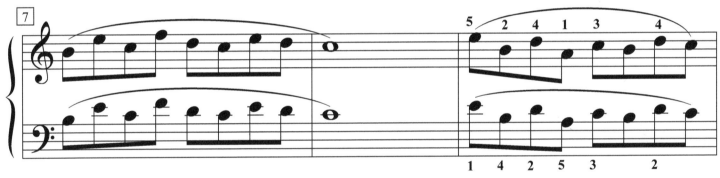

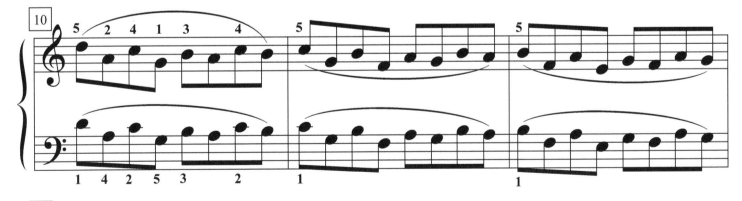

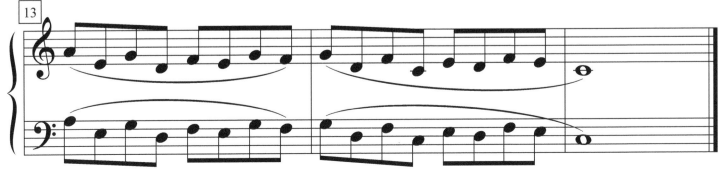

6. Trill (Ascending)

TRACK 11: Slow
TRACK 12: Tempo

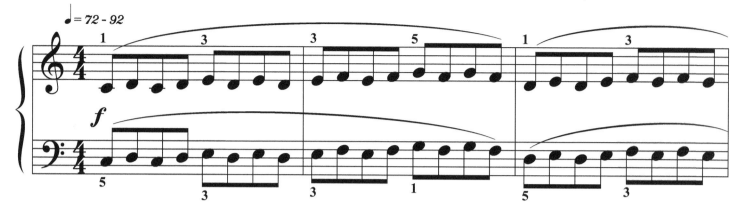

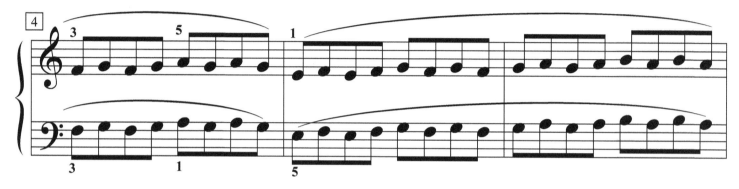

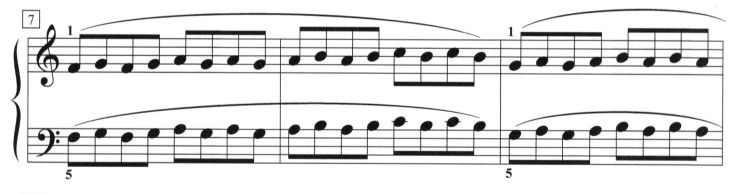

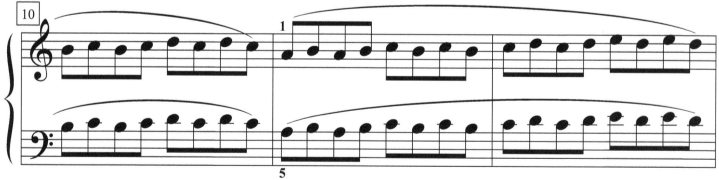

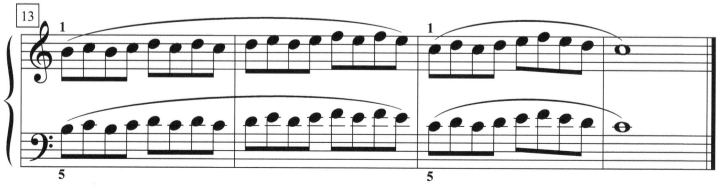

NOTE: It is recommended that the student accent the 1st and 3rd counts of of each measure.

7. Trill (Descending)

TRACK 13: Slow
TRACK 14: Tempo

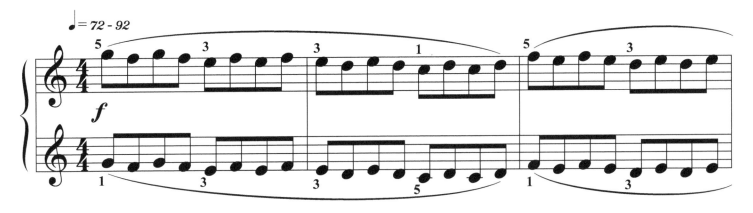

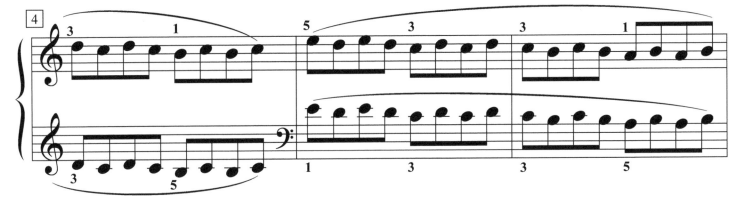

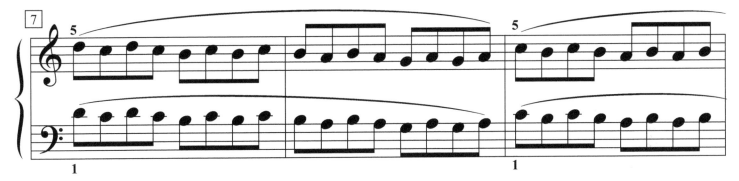

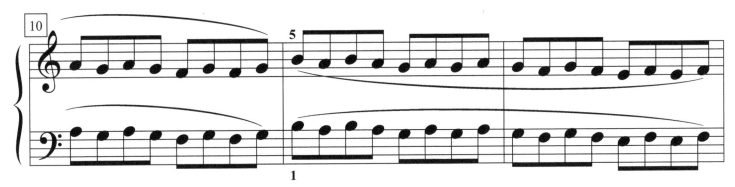

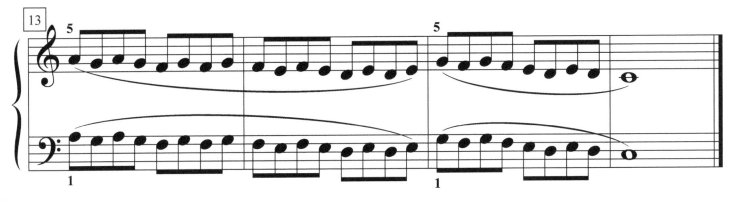

8. Syncopation on Second Count

TRACK 15: Slow
TRACK 16: Tempo

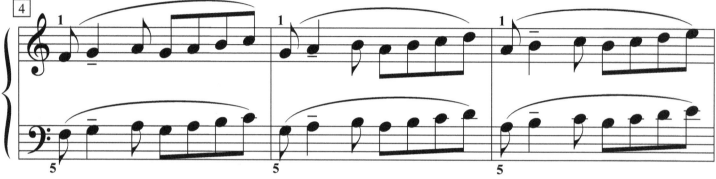

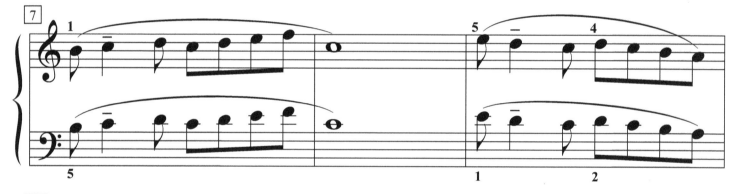

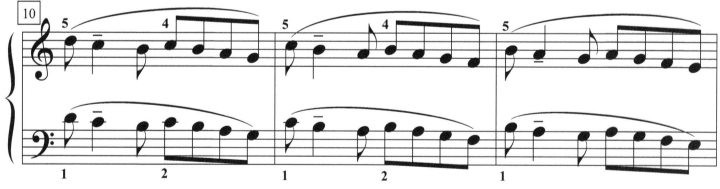

9. Syncopation on Third Count

TRACK 17: Slow
TRACK 18: Tempo

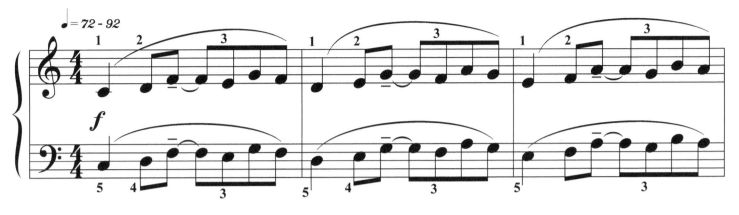

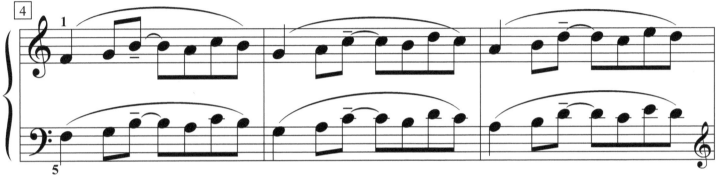

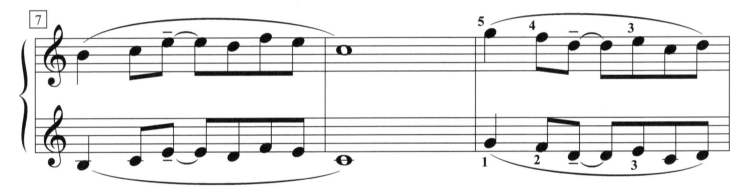

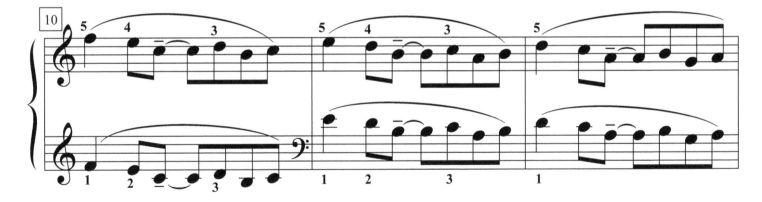

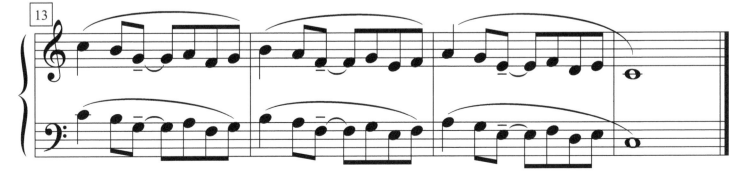

10. Syncopation on Fourth Count

TRACK 19: Slow
TRACK 20: Tempo

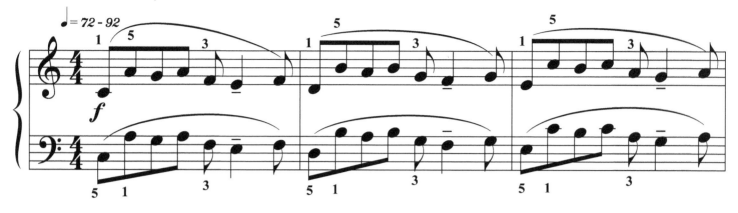

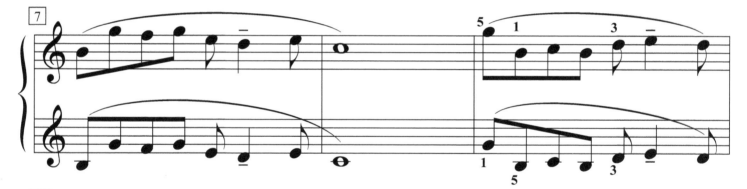

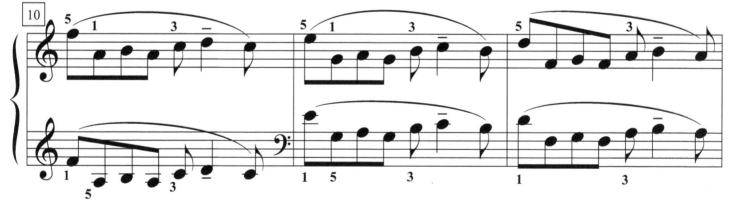

11. Wrist Staccato

TRACK 21: Slow
TRACK 22: Tempo

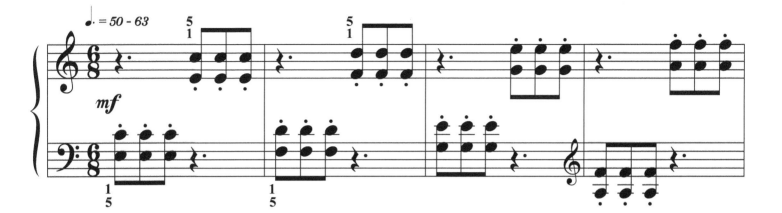

12. Wrist Rotation

TRACK 23: Slow
TRACK 24: Tempo

DIRECTIONS: Also play this study with the following finger patterns:

$$\begin{cases} \textbf{R.H.} \ 2\text{-}4\text{-}2\text{-}4\text{-}2\text{-}4 \\ \textbf{L.H.} \ 4\text{-}2\text{-}4\text{-}2\text{-}4\text{-}2 \end{cases} \qquad \begin{cases} \textbf{R.H.} \ 3\text{-}5\text{-}3\text{-}5\text{-}3\text{-}5 \\ \textbf{L.H.} \ 5\text{-}3\text{-}5\text{-}3\text{-}5\text{-}3 \end{cases}$$

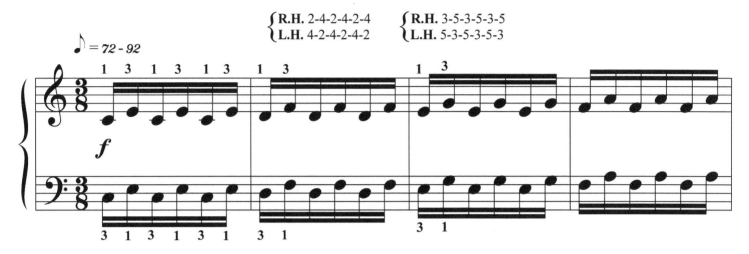

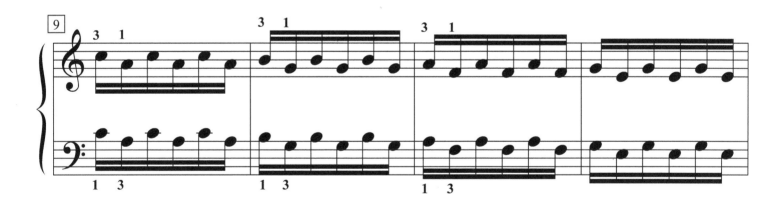

13. Rotation Etude

TRACK 25: Slow
TRACK 26: Tempo

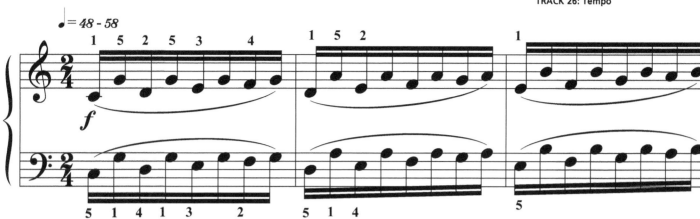

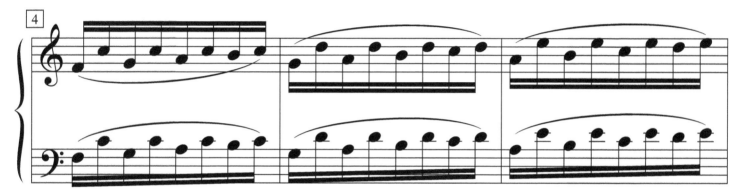

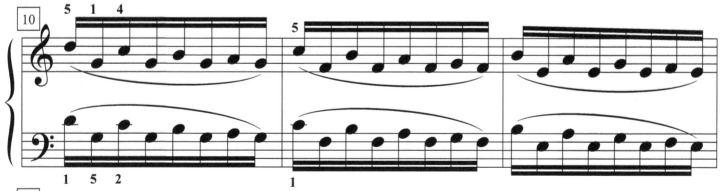

14. Hand Expansion (2/4)

TRACK 27: Slow
TRACK 28: Tempo

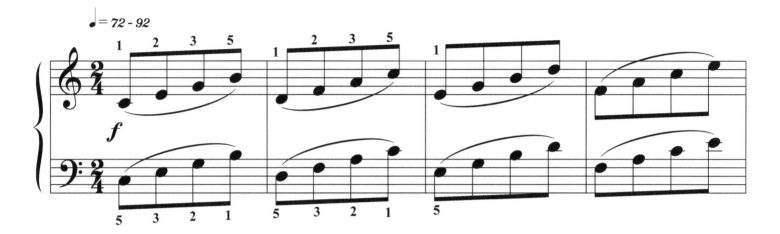

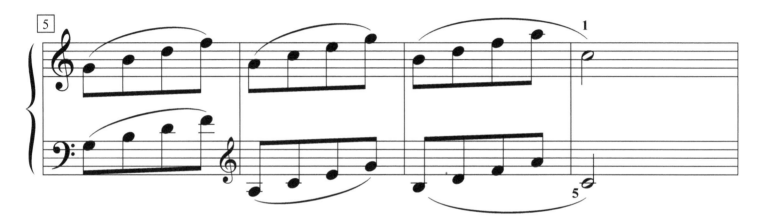

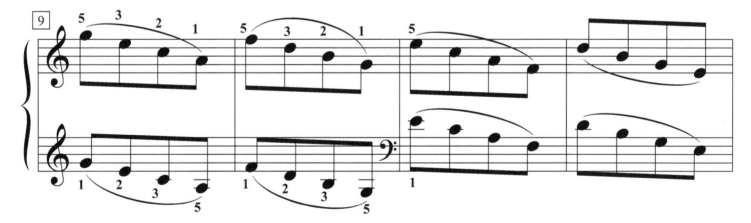

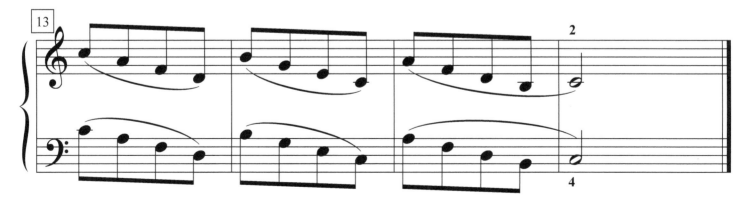

15. Hand Expansion (3/4)

TRACK 29: Slow
TRACK 30: Tempo

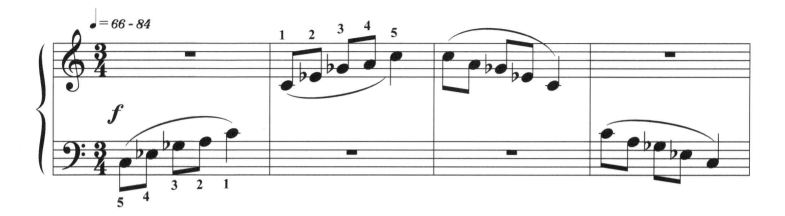

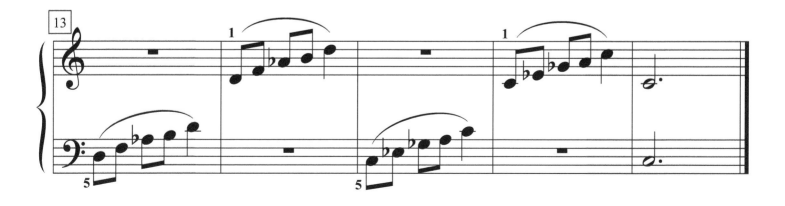

16. Thumb Crossing

TRACK 31: Slow
TRACK 32: Tempo

DIRECTIONS: Also play this study with the following finger patterns:

$\begin{cases} \textbf{R.H.} \ 1\text{-}3\text{-}1\text{-}3\text{-}1\text{-}3 \\ \textbf{L.H.} \ 1\text{-}3\text{-}1\text{-}3\text{-}1\text{-}3 \end{cases}$ $\begin{cases} \textbf{R.H.} \ 1\text{-}4\text{-}1\text{-}4\text{-}1\text{-}4 \\ \textbf{L.H.} \ 1\text{-}4\text{-}1\text{-}4\text{-}1\text{-}4 \end{cases}$

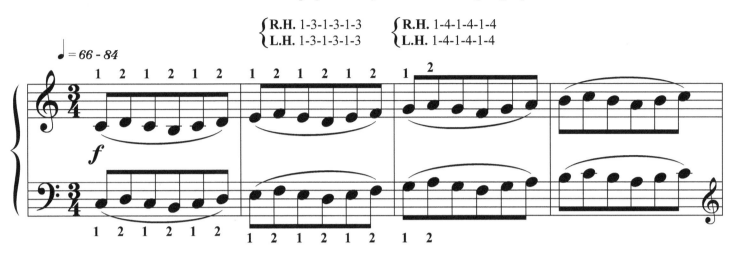

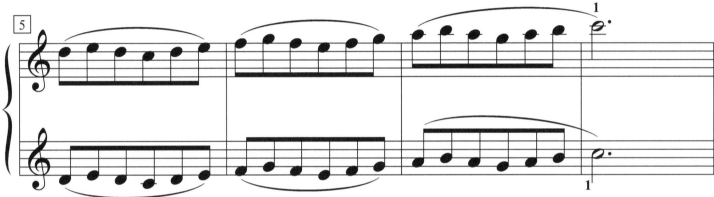

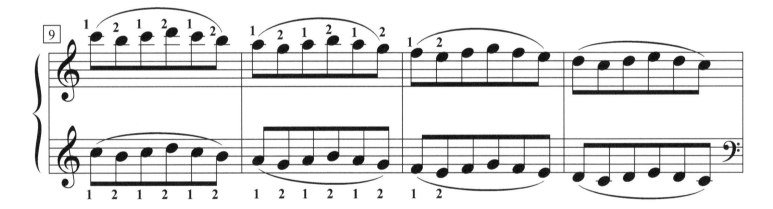

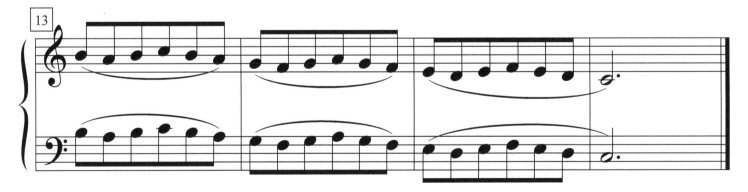

NOTE: It is recommended that the student practice this exercise with a quarter (coin) placed on the back of each hand.
This will aid in keeping the hands steady.

17. Scale Preparatory

TRACK 33: Slow
TRACK 34: Tempo

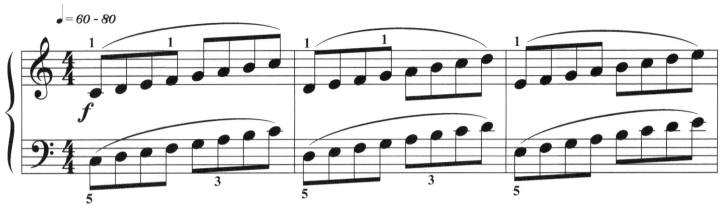

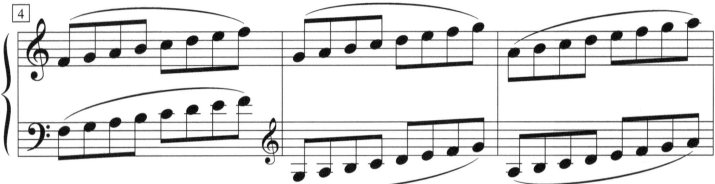

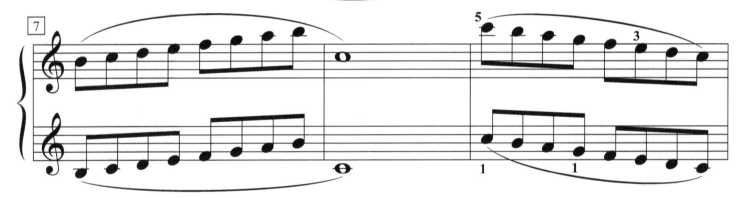

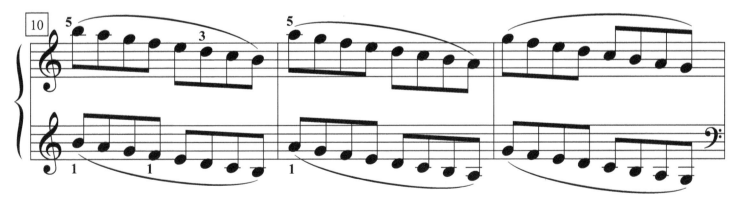

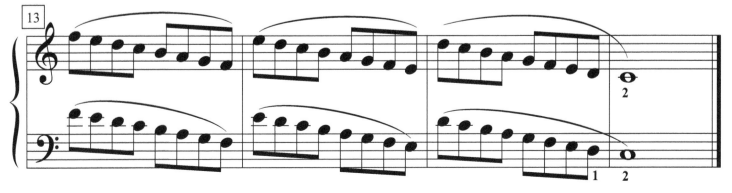

18. Chromatic Scale

TRACK 35: Slow
TRACK 36: Tempo

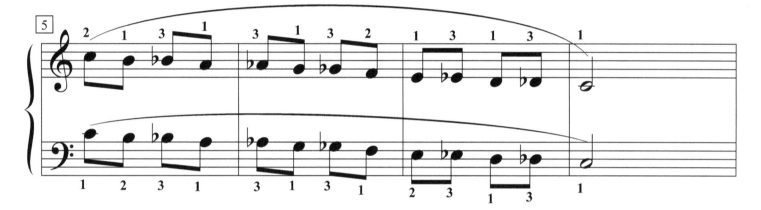

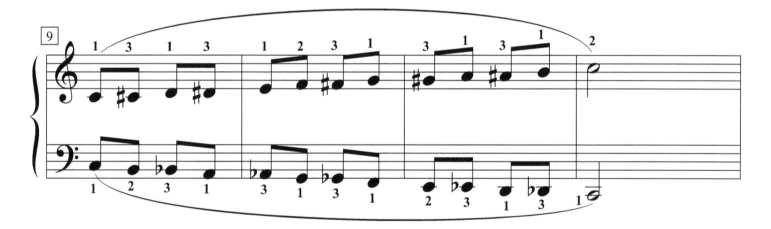

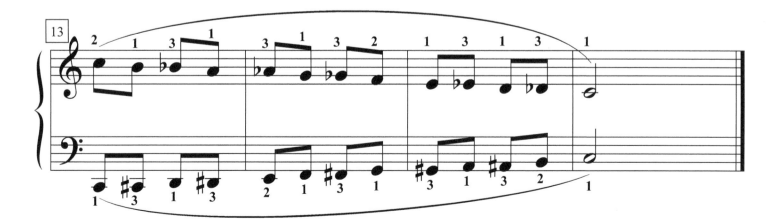

19. Chromatic Chord Progressions

TRACK 37: Slow
TRACK 38: Tempo

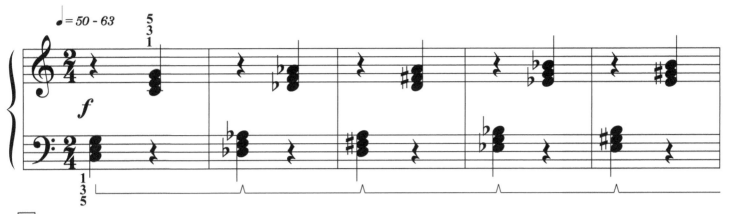

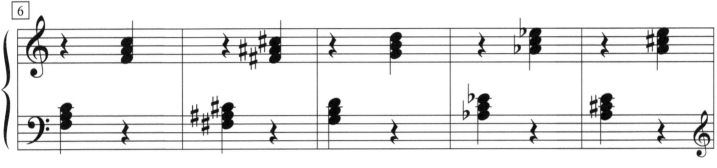

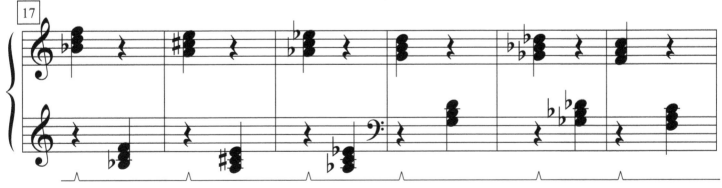

20. Chromatic Arpeggios (Ascending)

TRACK 39: Slow
TRACK 40: Tempo

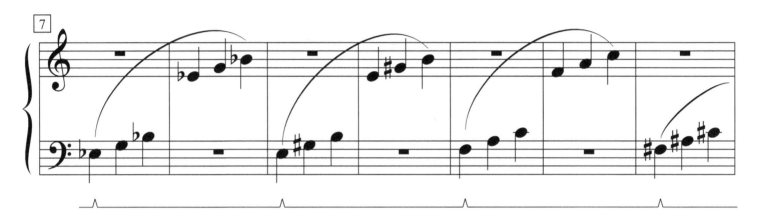

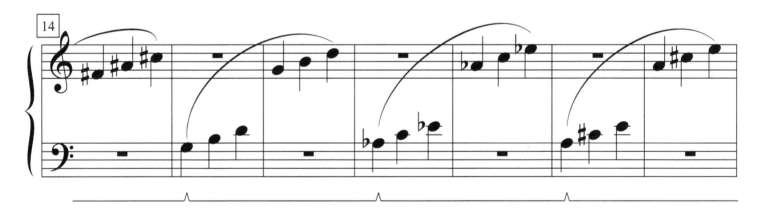

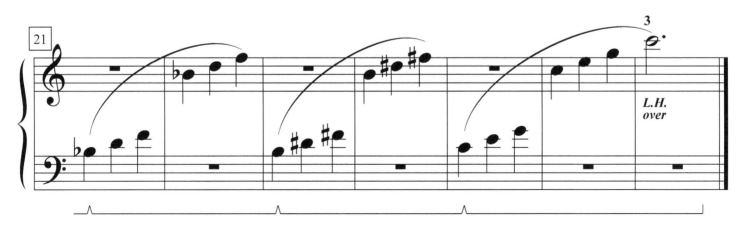

21. Chromatic Arpeggios (Descending)

TRACK 41: Slow
TRACK 42: Tempo

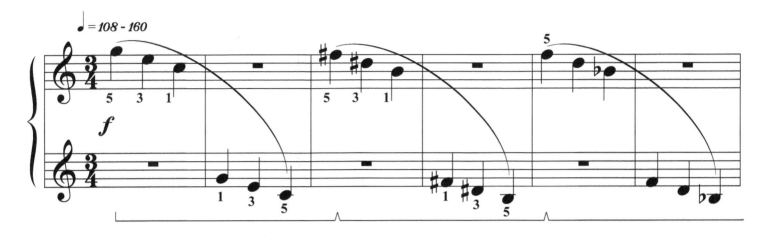

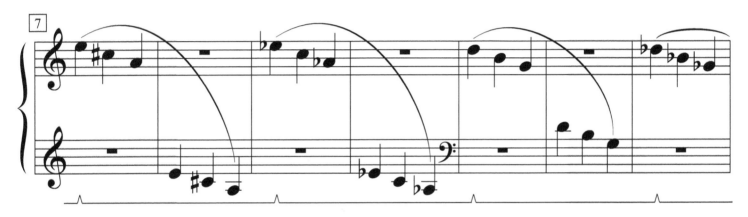

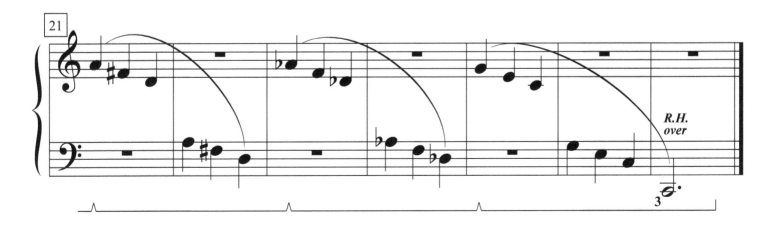

MORE GREAT SCHAUM PUBLICATIONS

FINGERPOWER®

by John W. Schaum

Physical training and discipline are needed for both athletics and keyboard playing. Keyboard muscle conditioning is called technic. Technic exercises are as important to the keyboard player as workouts and calisthenics are to the athlete. Schaum's *Fingerpower* books are dedicated to development of individual finger strength and dexterity in both hands.

00645334 Primer Level – Book Only $6.99
00645016 Primer Level –
            Book/Audio $8.99
00645335 Level 1 – Book Only $6.99
00645019 Level 1 – Book/Audio . . . $7.99
00645336 Level 2 – Book Only $6.99
00645022 Level 2 – Book/Audio . . . $7.99
00645337 Level 3 – Book Only $6.95
00645025 Level 3 – Book/Audio . . . $7.99
00645338 Level 4 – Book Only $6.99
00645028 Level 4 – Book/Audio . . . $8.99
00645339 Level 5 Book Only $6.99
00645340 Level 6 Book Only $6.99

FINGERPOWER® ETUDES

Melodic exercises crafted by master technic composers. Modified or transposed etudes provide equal hand development with a planned variety of technical styles, key, and time signatures.

00645392 Primer Level $6.95
00645393 Level 1 . . . . $6.99
00645394 Level 2 . . . . $6.99
00645395 Level 3 . . . . $6.95
00645396 Level 4 . . . . $6.99

FINGERPOWER® FUN

arr. Wesley Schaum
Early Elementary Level

Musical experiences beyond the traditional *Fingerpower* books that include fun to play pieces with finger exercises and duet accompaniments. Short technic prepatory drills (finger workouts) focus on melodic patterns found in each piece.

00645126 Primer Level $6.95
00645127 Level 1 . . . . $6.95
00645128 Level 2 . . . . $6.95
00645129 Level 3 . . . . $6.95
00645144 Level 4 . . . . $6.95

FINGERPOWER POP

Arranged by James Poteat

10 great pop piano solo arrangements with fun technical warm-ups that complement the Fingerpower series! Can also be used as motivating supplements to any method and in any learning situation.

00237508 Primer Level $9.99
00237510 Level 1 . . . . $9.99
00282865 Level 2 . . . . $9.99

FINGERPOWER® TRANSPOSER

by Wesley Schaum
Early Elementary Level

This book includes 21 short, 8-measure exercises using 5-finger patterns. Positions are based on C,F, and G major and no key signatures are used. Patterns involve intervals of 3rds, 4ths, and 5ths up and down and are transposed from C to F and F to C, C to G and G to C, G to F and F to G.

00645150 Primer Level $6.95
00645151 Level 1 . . . . $6.95
00645152 Level 2 . . . . $6.95
00645154 Level 3 . . . . $6.95
00645156 Level 4 . . . . $6.95

JUMBO STAFF MANUSCRIPT BOOK

This pad features 24 pages with 4 staves per page.
00645936 . . . . $4.25

CERTIFICATE OF MUSICAL ACHIEVEMENT

Reward your students for their hard work with these official 8x10 inch certificates that you can customize. 12 per package.
00645938 . . . . $6.99

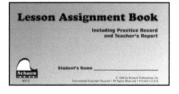

SCHAUM LESSON ASSIGNMENT BOOK

by John Schaum

With space for 32 weeks, this book will help keep students on the right track for their practice time.
00645935 . . . . $3.95

www.halleonard.com

0519